MEMORANDA

ON

SHAKESPEARE'S COMEDY

OF

MEASURE FOR MEASURE

AMS PRESS

NEW YORK

MEMORANDA

ON

SHAKESPEARE'S COMEDY

OF

MEASURE FOR MEASURE.

BY

J. O. HALLIWELL-PHILLIPPS.

LONDON.

PRINTED IN THE YEAR 1880.

Library of Congress Cataloging in Publication Data

Halliwell-Phillipps, James Orchard, 1820—1889.
    Memoranda on Shakespeare's comedy of Measure for
measure.

    1. Shakespeare, William, 1564—1616. Measure for
measure. I. Title.
PR2824.H3 1974   822.3'3   74-168226
ISBN 0-404-03068-8

Reprinted from the edition of 1880, London
First AMS edition published, 1974
Manufactured in the United States of America

AMS PRESS, INC.
New York, N.Y. 10003

MEMORANDA.

"THEY report a historie of one who did yet worse. It was the Provost *la Vouste*, who plaied a wicked part with a certaine honest woman. She comming unto him to make sute for her husband, whom this Provost kept in prison, was required to graunt him one nights pleasure, and he would yield to whatsoever shee herselfe demanded. This woman, finding herselfe much perplexed, looking on the one side to her breach of faith plighted to her husband, and on the other side his life which she should save, shee was very desirous to acquaint her husband therewith ; who, having dispenced there-withall, shee then yields unto the Provosts brutish desire, resting assured that he would certainly keepe promise with her concerning her husband. But in the morning this most vilde wretch, after he had caused her husband to be hanged, said thus unto her,—I did promise, indeede, to restore you your husband ; I keepe him not, but I yield him unto you," Goulart's Admirable and Memorable Histories, 4to. 1607.

Reed, speaking of Heywood's Woman Kill'd with Kindness, acted in 1602, observes that " the pleadings of Sir Charles with his sister to give up her person to Acton for the discharge of his debt and ransom of his liberty, and her reflections on the proposal, seem borrowed in some degree from the scenes between Claudio and Isabella in Measure for Measure ;" but if there is any imitation at all, it was probably on the side of the great dramatist.

The real meaning of Overdone, appropriately applied to a bawd, must be referred to a licentious use of *done*, from *do* in a luxurious sense. *Over-doing* is used in a similar manner in the Women's Advocate, 1683, p. 44. There is a Mrs. Overdon in Dryden's Kind Keeper, 1680, p. 37.

The allusion to Pompey's hose in the second Act is thus commented on by Steevens,—" in consequence of a diligent inspection of ancient pictures and prints, it may be pronounced that this ridiculous fashion appeared in the early part of Elizabeth's reign, then declined, and recommenced at the beginning of that of James the First." If this view can be sustained, here would be an evidence in favour of placing the comedy early in the reign of James the First.

In Lupton's Second Part and Knitting Up of the Boke entituled Too Good to be True, 1581, there is a story related of a

judge who induced a lady to pass the night
with him, and to pay him also six thousand
crowns, for the sake of preserving her
husband from execution. Notwithstanding
the lady's compliance with his demands, her
husband was executed, but she succeeded in
proving the judge's guilt to the satisfaction
of a superior court, and her betrayer was
sentenced to marry her, but was executed
immediately after the ceremony was performed. As the judge's widow, she thus
became entitled to the whole of his property.
The story itself is not worth quoting.

Both stanzas of the song, " Take, oh take
those lips away," are given with the initials
W. S. in a manuscript of the seventeenth
century in the British Museum, MS. Harl.
6057, fol. 36, but it is not likely that there
is here any good evidence of authorship.

" In the yere 1547 a citizen of Comun
was cast into prison upon an accusation of
murder, whom to deliver from the judge-

ment of death his wife wrought all means possible. Therefore, comming to the captaine that held him prisoner, she sued to him for her husbands life, who, upon condition of her yeelding to his lust and payment of 200 ducats, promised safe deliverance for him. The poore woman, seeing that nothing could redeeme her husbands life but losse and shipwracke of her owne honestie, told her husband, who willed her to yeeld to the captains desire and not to pretermit so good an occasion; wherefore she consented; but after the pleasure past, the traiterous and wicked captaine put her husband to death notwithstanding," Beard's Theatre of God's Judgements, 1612.

Froth the Tapster occurs in a list of similar names in Taylor's World Runnes on Wheeles, printed in the Workes, ed. 1630.

Measure for Measure was certainly in existence in December, 1604. In the old transcripts of the Audit Accounts made for

Malone is the following,—" 1604 and 1605. Ed. Tylney.   On   St.   Stephens   night, Mesure for Mesur by Shaxberd, performed by the K.'s players."

There is surely a mistake in the statement that William Barksted acted with the King's Company.   The evidences in my possession clearly show that he never did. Malone obscurely says that he " was employed in the theatre where our author's plays were represented."

Twenty Copies Printed.
December, 1880.

Chiswick Press :

C. WHITTINGHAM AND CO. TOOKS COURT,

CHANCERY LANE.

Number **Thirteen.**